Success an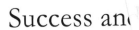

Quot...

Motivate

Inspire

&

Live by

Atticus Aristotle

DEDICATION

This book is dedicated to the teachers who showed me that true happiness lies in doing things you love, and accepting yourself for who you are, not for who others want you to be.

Table of Contents

Introduction

Achieving happiness is not about acquiring what we seek. Happiness is being at peace with what you have. Happiness is a frame of mind, easy to achieve just by thinking and behaving differently. The aim of this book is to help you achieve happiness by showing you how to release the inner you, the 'you' that's unburdened with the weight of the world. The phrases and sayings within this book are intended to motivate, inspire and help lead you towards a contented and fulfilled state of mind, towards happiness.

The phrases and sayings included in this book were chosen because they provide guidance for the individual, rather than abstract sayings intended for the masses.

The phrases and sayings are grouped by topics relevant to you. The best way to use this book is to review the chapters, then turn to the one which fits in best with the mood you're in, or dilemma you're facing at the time. Keep it nearby, so when doubt, stress, uncertainty or anything else comes along which causes you to pause, go to the appropriate chapter. Look down the list and you will find an appropriate phrase or saying to calm you and help guide you towards the right action, or frame of mind

Honesty and Truth

The precepts of the law are these: to live honestly, to injure no one, and to give every man his due.

Justinian I

A promise made is a debt unpaid.

Robert W. Service

Frankness invites frankness.

Ralph Waldo Emerson

We must not promise what we ought not, lest we be called on to perform what we cannot.

Abraham Lincoln

The truth is not always the same as the majority decision.

Pope John Paul II (Karol Wojtyla)

Don't tell your friends their social faults; they will cure the fault and never forgive you.

Logan Pearsall Smith

An overdose of praise is like 10 lumps of sugar in coffee; only a very few people can swallow it.

Emily Post

Honesty is not a policy, it is a state of mind.

Eugene LHote

When all else fails, tell the truth.

Donald T. Regan

A lie has speed, but truth has endurance.

Edgar J. Mohn

If you add to the truth, you subtract from it.

The Talmud

The most faithful mirror is an old friend.

Spanish proverb

A belief is not true because it is useful.

Henri Amiel

Lying can never save us from another lie.

Vaclav Havel

Time, whose tooth gnaws away at everything else, is powerless against truth.

Thomas Henry Huxley

It is better to be hated for what you are than to be loved for what you are not.

Andre Gide

Did ever a man try heroism, magnanimity, truth, sincerity, and find that there was no advantage in them -- that it was a vain endeavor?

Henry David Thoreau

Every kind of peaceful cooperation among men is primarily based on mutual trust and only secondarily on institutions such as courts of justice and police.

Albert Einstein

What you don't see with your eyes, don't witness with your mouth.

Jewish proverb

Whatever else may be shaken, there are some facts established beyond warring: virtue is better than vice, truth is better than falsehood, kindness than brutality.

Quintin Hogg

The greatest truths are the simplest, and so are the greatest men.

J.C. Hare

It is more shameful to distrust ones friends than to be deceived by them.

Francois duc de la Rochefoucauld

The pursuit of truth will set you free even if you never catch up with it.

Clarence Darrow

Most of our faults are more pardonable than the means we use to conceal them.

Francois duc de la Rochefoucauld

It takes less time to do a thing right than to explain why you did it wrong.

Henry Wadsworth Longfellow

The way to overcome the angry man is with gentleness, the evil man with goodness, the miser with generosity and the liar with truth.

Indian proverb

Karma

You can easily judge the character of a man by how he treats those who can do nothing for him.

Johann Wolfgang von Goethe

Parents wonder why the streams are bitter, when they themselves have poisoned the fountain.

John Locke

The value of marriage is not that adults produce children but that children produce adults.

Peter de Vries

Expecting the world to treat you fairly because you are a good person is a little like expecting the bull not to attack you because you are a vegetarian.

Dennis Wholey

I have found that if you love life, life will love you back.

Arthur Rubinstein

Mine honour is my life; both grow in one; Take honour from me, and my life is done.

William Shakespeare

The liars punishment is not in the least that he is not believed, but that he cannot believe anyone else.

George Bernard Shaw

The jealous are troublesome to others, but torment to themselves.

William Penn

Do good with what thou hast, or it will do thee no good.

William Penn

Thoughts lead on to purposes; purposes go forth in action; actions form habits; habits decide character; and character fixes our destiny.

Unknown

They who give have all things; they who withhold have nothing.

Hindu proverb

Those who are free of resentful thoughts surely find peace.

Buddha (Siddhartha Gautama)

No man is more cheated than a selfish man.

Henry Ward Beecher

Our life is what our thoughts make it.

Marcus Aurelius

Act so as to elicit the best in others and thereby in thyself.

Felix Adler

People pay for what they do, and still more, for what they have allowed themselves to become. And they pay for it simply: by the lives they lead.

Edith Wharton

Doubt breeds doubt.

Franz Grillparzer

We are shaped and fashioned by what we love.

Johann Wolfgang von Goethe

If you keep on saying things are going to be bad, you have a good chance of becoming a prophet.

Isaac Bashevis Singer

To sensible men, every day is a day of reckoning.

John W. Gardner

The words you speak today should be soft and tender ... for tomorrow you may have to eat them.

Unknown

Hatred is blind, anger is foolhardy, and he who pours out vengeance risks having to drink a bitter draft.

Alexandre Dumas

When the Great Scorer comes to mark against your name, He writes not that you won or lost, but how you played the Game.

Grantland Rice

Let no man be sorry he has done good because others have done evil. If a man has acted right he has done well, though alone. If wrong, the sanction of all mankind will not justify him.

Henry Fielding

Cheat the earth and the earth will cheat you.

Chinese proverb

If you want happiness for an hour; take a nap. If you want happiness for a day; go fishing. If you want happiness for a month; get married. If you want happiness for a year; inherit a fortune. If you want happiness for a lifetime; help someone else.

Chinese proverb

Ethics and Morality

If it is not right do not do it; if it is not true do
not say it.

Marcus Aurelius

A man without ethics is a wild beast loosed
upon this world.

Albert Camus

Divorced from ethics, leadership is reduced to
management and politics to mere technique.

James MacGregor Burns

Bear the blame for your behavior.

Price Pritchett

Action indeed is the sole medium of
expression for ethics.

Jane Addams

Ethics and equity and the principles of justice
do not change with the calendar.

David Herbert Lawrence

Ethics is knowing the difference between what
you have a right to do and what is right to do.

Potter Stewart

Ethics is nothing else than reverence for life.

Albert Schweitzer

I can do no other than be reverent before
everything that is called life. I can do no other
than to have compassion for all that is called
life. That is the beginning and the foundation
of all ethics.

Albert Schweitzer

If you look to lead, invest at least 40% of your time managing yourself - your ethics, character, principles, purpose, motivation, and conduct. Invest at least 30% managing those with authority over you, and 15% managing your peers.

Dee Hock

More often there's a compromise between ethics and expediency.

Peter Singer

Our very lives depend on the ethics of strangers, and most of us are always strangers to other people.

Bill Moyers

The act of willing this or that, of choosing among various courses of conduct, is central in the realm of ethics.

Corliss Lamont

The first step in the evolution of ethics is a sense of solidarity with other human beings.
Albert Schweitzer

In this world everything changes except good deeds and bad deeds; these follow you as the shadow follows the body.
Unknown

The intention makes the crime.
Aristotle

If ethics are poor at the top, that behavior is copied down through the organization.
Robert Noyce

Lying and stealing are next-door neighbors.
Arab proverb

Life is the sum of your choices.
Albert Camus

Freedom is not procured by a full enjoyment of what is desired, but by controlling that desire.

Epictetus

Like the body that is made up of different limbs and organs, all moral creatures must depend on each other to exist.

Hindu proverb

To educate a person in mind and not in morals is to educate a menace to society.

Theodore Roosevelt

The best way to teach morality is to make it a habit with children.

Aristotle

Morality is simply the attitude we adopt toward people whom we personally dislike.

Oscar Wilde

The foundation of morality is to have done,
once and for all, with lying.

Thomas Henry Huxley

Whoever fights monsters should see to it that
in the process he does not become a monster.

Friedrich Nietzsche

A moral being is one who is capable of
comparing his past and future actions or
motives, and of approving or disapproving of
them.

Charles Darwin

Without civic morality communities perish;
without personal morality their survival has
no value.

Bertrand Russell

Ethics is a code of values which guide our
choices and actions and determine the
purpose and course of our lives.

Ayn Rand

Morality is stronger than tyrants.

Louis-Antoine-Leon de Saint-Just

All that we are is the result of what we have thought. If people speak or act with evil thoughts, pain follows them. If people speak or act with pure thoughts, happiness follows them, like a shadow that never leaves them.

Siddhartha Gautama

Few men have virtue to withstand the highest bidder.

George Washington

Compassion is the basis of morality.

Arthur Schopenhauer

Shelving hard decisions is the least ethical course.

Adrian Cadbury

Integrity

All paths lead to the same goal: to convey to others what we are.

Pablo Neruda

All bad precedents begin as justifiable measures.

Julius Caesar

Be as you wish to seem.

Socrates

The house of delusions is cheap to build but drafty to live in.

A.E. Housman

The hottest places in Hell are reserved for those who remain neutral in time of great moral crisis.

Dante Alighieri

Integrity without knowledge is weak and useless, and knowledge without integrity is dangerous and dreadful.

Samuel Johnson

Friendship with oneself is all-important, because without it one cannot be friends with anyone else.

Eleanor Roosevelt

In looking for people to hire, look for three qualities: integrity, intelligence and energy. And if they don't have the first, the other two will kill you.

Warren Buffet

Loyalty oaths increase the number of liars.

Noel Peattie

You can preach a better sermon with your life than with your lips.

Oliver Goldsmith

Everyone thinks of changing the world, but no one thinks of changing himself.

Count Leo Tolstoy

When speculation has done its worst, two and two still make four.

Samuel Johnson

Of all the paths a man could strike into, there is, at any given moment, a best path. . . a thing which, here and now, it were of all things wisest for him to do ... to find his path and walk in it.

Thomas Carlyle

A man cannot be comfortable without his own approval.

Mark Twain (Samuel Clemens)

Men can starve from a lack of self-realization
as much as they can from a lack of bread.

Richard Wright

More people are flattered into virtue than
bullied out of vice.

Robert Smith Surtees

What people call the spirit of the times is
mostly their own spirit in which the times
mirror themselves.

Johann Wolfgang von Goethe

Never esteem anything as of advantage to you
that will make you break your word or lose
your self-respect.

Marcus Aurelius

People may fail many times, but they become
failures only when they begin to blame
someone else.

Unknown

Any man's life will be filled with constant and unexpected encouragement if he makes up his mind to do his level best each day.

Booker T. Washington

There are two kinds of people: those who do the work and those who take the credit. Try to be in the first group; there is less competition there.

Indira Gandhi

Always imitate the behavior of the winner when you lose.

Anonymous

Nature never deceives us; it is always we who deceive ourselves.

Jean-Jacques Rousseau

He that falls in love with himself will have no rivals.

Benjamin Franklin

He who conquers others is strong; he who conquers himself is mighty.

Lao-Tzu

Good habits result from resisting temptation.

Portuguese proverb

A wise man makes his own decisions; the ignorant goes with the crowd.

Chinese proverb

Before you make any decision, consider its effect on the next seven generations.

Hopi proverb

If you are an anvil, be patient; if you are a hammer, be strong.

Kurdish proverb

Once the 'what' is decided, the 'how' always follows. We must not make the 'how' an excuse for not facing and accepting the 'what.'

Pearl S. Buck

Know thyself.

Inscription at the Oracle of Delphi in ancient Greece

Character

Of all the properties which belong to honorable men, not one is so highly prized as that of character.

Henry Clay

Most people say that it is the intellect which makes a great scientist. They are wrong: it is character.

Albert Einstein

Character is what you are in the dark.

Unknown

Fame is a vapor, popularity an accident, riches take wing, and only character endures.
Horace Greeley

What lies behind us and what lies before us are small matters compared to what lies within us.
Ralph Waldo Emerson

If you will think about what you ought to do for other people, your character will take care of itself. Character is a by-product, and any man who devotes himself to its cultivation in his own case will become a selfish prig.
Woodrow Wilson

We are what we seem to be.
Willard Gaylin

What someone is, begins to be revealed when his talent abates, when he stops showing us what he can do.
Friedrich Nietzsche

Character is like a tree and reputation like its shadow. The shadow is what we think of it; the tree is the real thing.

Abraham Lincoln

The function of education is to teach one to think intensively and to think critically... Intelligence plus character? That is the goal of true education.

Martin Luther King Jr.

Character cannot be developed in ease and quiet. Only through experience of trial and suffering can the soul be strengthened, vision cleared, ambition inspired, and success achieved.

Helen Keller

Character is that which reveals moral purpose, exposing the class of things a man chooses and avoids.

Aristotle

The measure of a man's character is what he would do if he knew he never would be found out.

Baron Thomas Babington Macauley

Character, in the long run, is the decisive factor in the life of an individual and of nations alike.

Theodore Roosevelt

The proper time to influence the character of a child is about a hundred years before he's born.

William R. Inge

If we want our children to possess the traits of character we most admire, we need to teach them what those traits are and why they deserve both admiration and allegiance. Children must learn to identify the forms and content of those traits.

William J. Bennett

The formation of character in young people is educationally a different task from and a prior task to, the discussion of the great, difficult ethical controversies of the day.

William J. Bennett

Conviction is worthless unless it is converted into conduct.

Thomas Carlyle

Character is much easier kept than recovered.

Thomas Paine

Every man has three characters: that which he shows, that which he has, and that which he thinks he has.

Alphonse Karr

All paths lead to the same goal: to convey to others what we are.

Pablo Neruda

A man's character is his fate.

Heraclitus

Character is simply habit long continued.

Plutarch

One can acquire everything in solitude except character.

Henri Stendahl

No change of circumstances can repair a defect of character.

Ralph Waldo Emerson

The force of character is cumulative.

Ralph Waldo Emerson

Not in time, place or circumstance but in the man lies success.

James Joyce

It is with trifles, and when he is off guard, that a man best reveals his character.

Arthur Schopenhauer

If a man has any greatness in him, it comes to light, not in one flamboyant hour, but in the ledger of his daily work.

Beryl Markham

Since the things we do determine the character of life, no blessed person can become unhappy, for he will never do those things which are hateful and petty.

Aristotle

Weakness of attitude becomes weakness of character.

Albert Einstein

Character is power.

Booker T. Washington

Nearly all men can stand adversity, but if you want to test a man's character, give him power.

Abraham Lincoln

Simplicity of character is no hindrance to the subtlety of intellect.

John Morley

To finish the moment, to find the journey's end in every step of the road, to live the greatest number of good hours, is wisdom.

Ralph Waldo Emerson

When you are content to be simply yourself and don't compare or compete, everybody will respect you.

Lao-Tzu

We can really respect a man only if he doesn't always look out for himself.

Johann Wolfgang von Goethe

All bullies are cowards, and most cowards are bullies.

Proverb

The weak can never forgive. Forgiveness is the attribute of the strong.

Mohandas Gandhi

If you tell the truth, you don't have to remember anything.

Mark Twain (Samuel Clemens)

A good reputation is something you must pay for, but you can never buy.

African proverb

If there is beauty in character, there will be harmony in the home. If there is harmony in the home, there will be order in the nation. If there is order in the nation, there will be peace in the world.

Chinese proverb

One minute of patience can result in ten years of peace.

Italian proverb

Failure is the mother of success.
> Chinese proverb

Decide on what you think is right, and stick to it.
> George Eliot (Mary Anne Evans)

Life is not a continuum of pleasant choices, but of inevitable problems that call for strength, determination, and hard work.
> Indian proverb

Life is like a game of cards. The hand that is dealt you represents determinism; the way you play it is free will.
> Jawaharlal Nehru

Don't try to be different. Just be good. To be good is different enough.
> Arthur Freed

Laws control the lesser person. Right conduct controls the greater one.
> Chinese proverb

You are responsible for you.

English proverb

Love all, trust a few, do wrong to none.

William Shakespeare

Wise people care not for that which they
cannot have.

Italian proverb

True strength lies in gentleness.

Irish proverb

All that we are is the result of what we have
thought. If people speak or act with evil
thoughts, pain follows them. If people speak or
act with pure thoughts, happiness follows
them, like a shadow that never leaves them.

Siddhartha Gautama

Conscience

A clear conscience is a good pillow.

American Proverb

A guilty conscience needs no accuser.

Anonymous

The measure of a man's character is what he would do if he knew he never would be found out.

Baron Thomas Babington Macauley

Prudence reproaches; conscience accuses.

Immanuel Kant

If all the world hated you and believed you wicked, while your own conscience approved of you and absolved you from guilt, you would not be without friends.

Charlotte Bronte

Conscience is what makes a boy tell his mother before his sister does.

Evan Esar

Conscience is God's presence in man.

Emmanuel Swedenborg

Cowardice asks: Is it safe? Expediency asks: Is it politic? But Conscience asks: Is it right?

William Punshon

Reason often makes mistakes but conscience never does.

Josh Billings (Henry Wheeler Shaw)

Freedom is a clear conscience.

Periander

Conscience is thoroughly well-bred and soon leaves off talking to those who do not wish to hear it.

Samuel Butler

A regard for reputation and the judgment of the world may sometimes be felt where conscience is dormant.

Thomas Jefferson

The difficulty is to know conscience from self-interest.

William Dean Howells

There is no witness so terrible, no accuser so powerful as conscience which dwells within us.

Sophocles

There is no witness so dreadful, no accuser so terrible as the conscience that dwells in the heart of every man.

Polybius

A moral being is one who is capable of comparing his past and future actions or motives, and of approving or disapproving of them.

Charles Darwin

Rise above principle and do what is right.

Walter Heller

The greatest of faults, I should say, is to be conscious of none.

Thomas Carlyle

Think like a man of action, act like a man of thought.

Henri Bergson

He who steals an egg will steal a camel.

Arab proverb

Never do anything against conscience even if the state demands it.

Albert Einstein

Lying and stealing are next-door neighbors.
                                        Arab proverb

He who steals once is always a thief.
                                        Spanish proverb

It is not fair to ask of others what you are
unwilling to do yourself.
                                        Eleanor Roosevelt

Conscience is the voice of the soul.
                                        Polish Proverb

...the safest course is to do nothing against
one's conscience. With this secret, we can
enjoy life and have no fear from death.
                                        Voltaire

Every man, at the bottom of his heart, wants to
do right. But only he can do right who knows
right; only he knows right who thinks right;
only he thinks right who believes right.
                                        Tiorio

Rules of society are nothing; one's conscience is the umpire.

Marie Anne de Vichy-Chamrond

All a man can betray is his conscience.

Joseph Conrad

Labor to keep alive in your breast that little spark of celestial fire, called conscience.

George Washington

Fairness

It is less important to redistribute wealth than it is to redistribute opportunity.

Arthur Vandenberg

To blame is easy; to do it better is difficult.

German proverb

Examine what is said, not the person who speaks.

Native American proverb

A person who cheats at play will cheat you any way.

Dutch proverb

An onion shared with a friend tastes like roast lamb.

Egyptian proverb

A bad workman blames his tools.

Chinese proverb

If you cannot catch a fish, do not blame the sea.

Greek proverb

Charity doesn't excuse cheating.

Yiddish proverb

Though force can protect in emergency, only justice, fairness, consideration and cooperation can finally lead men to the dawn of eternal peace.

Dwight D. Eisenhower

Fairness is man's ability rise above his prejudices.

Wes Fessler

Gratitude is the least of virtues, but
ingratitude the worst of vices.

French proverb

Win or lose, do it fairly.

Knute Rockne

If my neighbor is happy, my own work will go
easier, too.

Macedonian proverb

We learn by watching and listening.

Japanese proverb

Entering a village, obey the village.

Japanese proverb

Lock your door rather than suspect your
neighbor.

Lebanese proverb

Having drunk the country's water, one should
obey the country's laws.

Tibetan proverb

Live so that when your children think of fairness, caring, and integrity, they think of you.

H. Jackson Brown, Jr.

It is not fair to ask of others what you are unwilling to do yourself

Eleanor Roosevelt

Do not complain of life's unfairness. It is never fair - at best it is impartial.

David Gemmell

Let the watchwords of all our people be the old familiar watchwords of honesty, decency, fair-dealing, and commonsense.... We must treat each man on his worth and merits as a man. We must see that each is given a square deal, because he is entitled to no more and should receive no less. The welfare of each of us is dependent fundamentally upon the welfare of all of us.

Teddy Roosevelt

In the end we are always rewarded for our good will, our patience, fair-mindedness, and gentleness with what is strange.

Friedrich Nietzsche

Principles & Values

In matters of style, swim with the current. In matters of principle, stand like a rock.

Thomas Jefferson

The time is always right to do what is right.

Martin Luther King

Never let your sense of morals prevent you from doing what is right.

Isaac Asimov

Control of mental conduct, not skill, is the sign of a matured samurai.

Japanese proverb

Whatever else may be shaken, there are some facts established beyond warring: virtue is better than vice, truth is better than falsehood, kindness than brutality.

Quintin Hogg

He that's cheated twice by the same man is an accomplice with the cheater.

Thomas Fuller

We become just by the practice of just actions, self-controlled by exercising self-control, and courageous by performing acts of courage.

Aristotle

Fortune lost, nothing lost; courage lost, much lost; honor lost, more lost; soul lost, all lost.

Dutch proverb

Two things fill my mind with ever-increasing wonder and awe: the starry heavens above me and the moral law within me.

Immanuel Kant

Don't approach a goat from the front, a horse from the back, or a fool from any side.

Jewish proverb

When wealth is lost, nothing is lost. When health is lost, something is lost; when character is lost, all is lost.

German proverb

A slave shows his true character, not while he is enslaved, but when he becomes a master.

Jewish proverb

We talk on principle but we act on interest.

William Savage Landor

As a man, I've been representative of the values I hold dear. And the values I hold dear are carryovers from the lives of my parents.

Sidney Poitier

It's easy to have principles when you're rich.
The important thing is to have principles
when you're poor.

Ray Kroc

Trust - Betrayal

The precepts of the law are these: to live honestly, to injure no one, and to give every man his due.

Justinian I

Frankness invites frankness.

Ralph Waldo Emerson

A lie has speed, but truth has endurance.

Edgar J. Mohn

We must not promise what we ought not, lest we be called on to perform what we cannot.

Abraham Lincoln

If you add to the truth, you subtract from it.

The Talmud

What you don't see with your eyes, don't
witness with your mouth.

Jewish proverb

Flattery makes friends, truth enemies.

Spanish proverb

It is more shameful to distrust ones friends
than to be deceived by them.

Francois duc de la Rochefoucauld

The liars punishment is not in the least that he
is not believed, but that he cannot believe
anyone else.

George Bernard Shaw

Most of our faults are more pardonable than
the means we use to conceal them.

Francois duc de la Rochefoucauld

How many times do you get to lie before you are a liar?

Michael Josephson

He who steals once is always a thief.

Spanish proverb

You may be deceived if you trust too much, but you will live in torment unless you trust enough.

Frank Crane

Charity never made poor, stealing never made rich, and wealth never made wise.

English Proverb

Who lies for you will lie against you.

Bosnian proverb

A thief is a thief, whether he steals a diamond or a cucumber.

Indian proverb

A single penny fairly got is worth a thousand
that are not.

German proverb

When spider webs unite, they can tie up a lion.

Ethiopian proverb

Good habits result from resisting temptation.

Portuguese proverb

Love all, trust a few, do wrong to none.

William Shakespeare

If you damage the character of another
person, you damage your own.

Yoruba proverb

It is better to be loved than feared.

Senegalese proverb

The way to overcome the angry man is with
gentleness, the evil man with goodness, the
miser with generosity and the liar with truth.

Indian proverb

Human Nature

We may pretend we are basically moral people who make mistakes, but the whole of history proves otherwise.

Terry Hands

Capitalism is the astounding belief that the most wickedest of men will do the most wickedest of things for the greatest good of everyone.

John Maynard Keynes

In order to exist, man must rebel.

Albert Camus

We are what we seem to be.

Willard Gaylin

Imagination was given to us to compensate for what we are not; a sense of humor was given to us to console us for what we are.

Mack McGinnis

Great occasions do not make heroes or cowards; they simply unveil them to the eyes. Silently and imperceptibly, as we wake or sleep, we grow strong or we grow weak, and at last some crisis shows us what we have become.

Brooke Foss Westcott

No one has yet fully realized the wealth of sympathy, kindness and generosity hidden in the soul of a child. The effort of every true education should be to unlock that treasure.

Emma Goldman

Morality is the best of all devices for leading mankind by the nose.

Friedrich Nietzsche

The belly comes before the soul.

George Orwell

False hope is worse than despair.

Jonathan Kozol

With our thoughts we make the world.

Buddha (Siddhartha Gautama)

Freedom and constraint are two aspects of the same necessity, the necessity of being the man you are and not another. You are free to be that man, but not another.

Antoine de Saint-Exupery

Our joys as winged dreams do fly; Why then should sorrow last? Since grief but aggravates thy loss, Grieve not for what is past.

Thomas Percy

Be happy. Talk happiness. Happiness calls out responsive gladness in others. There is enough sadness in the world without yours.... never doubt the excellence and permanence of what is yet to be. Join the great company of those who make the barren places of life fruitful with kindness.... Your success and happiness lie in you.... The great enduring realities are love and service.... Resolve to keep happy and your joy and you shall form an invincible host against difficulties.

Helen Keller

Happiness depends upon ourselves.

Aristotle

Welcome everything that comes to you, but do not long for anything else.

Andre Gide

All who would win joy, must share it; happiness was born a twin.

Lord Byron

If all our happiness is bound up entirely in our personal circumstances, it is difficult not to demand of life more than it has to give.

Bertrand Russell

Those who seek happiness, miss it, and those who discuss it, lack it.

Holbrook Jackson

Happiness is not the end of life: character is.

Henry Ward Beecher

Life is a comedy for those who think and a tragedy for those who feel.

Horace Walpole

In spite of everything, I still believe that people are really good at heart.

Anne Frank

There are two levers for moving men: interest and fear.

Napoleon Bonaparte

The tendency of mans nature to good is like
the tendency of water to flow downward.
Mencius (Meng-Tzu)

Resentment is like taking poison and waiting
for the other person to die.
Malachy McCourt

Everyone can master a grief but he that has it.
William Shakespeare

It is difficult to get a man to understand
something when his salary depends upon his
not understanding it.
Upton Sinclair

Necessity is an interpretation, not a fact.
Friedrich Nietzsche

Self-image sets the boundaries of individual
accomplishment.
Maxwell Maltz

To be nobody-but-yourself? in a world which is doing its best, night and day, to make you everybody else? means to fight the hardest battle which any human being can fight; and never stop fighting.

E. E. Cummings

Only the shallow know themselves.

Oscar Wilde

Of all the paths a man could strike into, there is, at any given moment, a best path. . . a thing which, here and now, it were of all things wisest for him to do ... to find his path and walk in it.

Thomas Carlyle

People pay for what they do, and still more, for what they have allowed themselves to become. And they pay for it simply: by the lives they lead.

Edith Wharton

When eating a fruit, think of the person who planted the tree.

Vietnamese saying

The beauty of the soul shines out when a man bears with composure one heavy mischance after another, not because he does not feel them, but because he is a man of high and heroic temper.

Aristotle

Anyone can become angry. That is easy, but to be angry with the right person, to the right degree, at the right time, for the right purpose, and in the right way? This is not easy.

Aristotle

A true history of human events would show that a far larger proportion of our acts are the results of sudden impulses and accident than of that reason of which we so much boast.

Peter Cooper

The greatest cunning is to have none at all.

French proverb

Do not use a hatchet to remove a fly from your friend's forehead.

Chinese proverb

With true friends...even water drunk together is sweet enough.

Chinese proverb

Pray to God, but keep rowing toward(s) the shore.

Chinese proverb

Do not want others to know what you have done? Better not have done it anyways.

Chinese proverb

Don't wrestle with pigs. You both get dirty and the pig likes it.

Mark Twain (Samuel Clemens)

What lies behind us and what lies before us are small matters compared to what lies within us.

Ralph Waldo Emerson

Character cannot be developed in ease and quiet. Only through experience of trial and suffering can the soul be strengthened, vision cleared, ambition inspired, and success achieved.

Helen Keller

The proper time to influence the character of a child is about a hundred years before he's born.

William R. Inge

Not in time, place or circumstance but in the man lies success.

James Joyce

Like the body that is made up of different limbs and organs, all moral creatures must depend on each other to exist.

Hindu proverb

What you are afraid to do is a clear indicator of the next thing you need to do.

Unknown

No wind favors he who has no destined port.

Michel de Montaigne

Happiness depends upon ourselves.

Aristotle

The value of marriage is not that adults produce children but that children produce adults.

Peter de Vries

Imitation is a necessity of human nature.

Oliver Wendell Holmes

But if you ask what is the good of education in general, the answer is easy: that education makes good men, and that good men act nobly.

Plato

Education makes a people easy to lead, but difficult to drive; easy to govern, but impossible to enslave.

Omar N. Bradley

The first step in the evolution of ethics is a sense of solidarity with other human beings.

Albert Schweitzer

Principles have no real force except when one is well fed.

Mark Twain (Samuel Clemens)

All that is necessary for evil to triumph is for good men to do nothing.

Edmund Burke

The sad truth is that most evil is done by people who never make up their minds to be good or evil.

Hannah Arendt

We either make ourselves happy or miserable. The amount of work is the same.

Carlos Castaneda

If we only wanted to be happy it would be easy; but we want to be happier than other people, which is almost always difficult, since we think them happier than they are.

Charles-Louis de Secondat Baron de Montesquieu

Great hopes make great men.

Thomas Fuller

One must think like a hero merely to behave like a decent human being.

May Sarton

See to do good, and you will find that
happiness will run after you.

James Freeman Clarke

A man can refrain from wanting what he has
not and cheerfully make the best of a bird in
the hand.

Seneca

Happiness does not depend on outward things,
but on the way we see them.

Count Leo Tolstoy

A great obstacle to happiness is expecting too
much happiness.

Bernard de Fontanelle

The greater part of our happiness or misery
depends on our dispositions, and not our
circumstances.

Martha Washington

Nine requisites for contented living: Health enough to make work a pleasure. Wealth enough to support your needs. Strength to battle with difficulties and overcome them. Grace enough to confess your sins and forsake them. Patience enough to toil until some good is accomplished. Charity enough to see some good in your neighbor. Love enough to move you to be useful to others. Faith enough to make real the things of God. Hope enough to remove all anxious fears concerning the future.

Johann Wolfgang von Goethe

To get up each morning with the resolve to be happy . . . is to set our own conditions to the events of each day. To do this is to condition circumstances instead of being conditioned by them.

Ralph Waldo Emerson

To perceive is to suffer.

Aristotle

Weakness of attitude becomes weakness of character.

Albert Einstein

Those who believe they can do something are probably right and so are those who believe they can't.

Unknown

If we were logical, the future would be bleak indeed. But we are more than logical. We are human beings, and we have faith and we have hope, and we can work.

Jacques Cousteau

Ideals are like stars; you will not succeed in touching them with your hands. But like the seafaring man on the desert of waters, you choose them as your guides, and following them you will reach your destiny.

Carl Schurz

No great deed is done by falterers who ask for certainty.

George Eliot (Mary Ann Evans)

True goodness springs from a man's own heart. All men are born good.

Confucius

It is silly to go on pretending that under the skin we are brothers. The truth is more likely that under the skin we are all cannibals, assassins, traitors, liars and hypocrites.

Henry Miller

There is no grief which time does not lessen and soften.

Cicero

New opinions are always suspected, and usually opposed, without any other reason but because they are not common.

John Locke

Few men think, yet all will have opinions.
George Berkeley

Do what you want to do... But want to do what you are doing. Be what you want to be... But want to be what you are.
Unknown

Be honorable yourself if you wish to associate with honorable people.
Welsh proverb

A man cannot be comfortable without his own approval.
Mark Twain (Samuel Clemens)

Men can starve from a lack of self-realization as much as they can from a lack of bread.
Richard Wright

Our life is what our thoughts make it.
Marcus Aurelius

Those people who are uncomfortable in themselves are disagreeable to others.

William Hazlitt

Whoever fights monsters should see to it that in the process he does not become a monster.

Friedrich Nietzsche

We are shaped and fashioned by what we love.

Johann Wolfgang von Goethe

Lives of great people remind us we can make our lives sublime and, departing, leave behind footprints in the sand of time.

Henry Wadsworth Longfellow

The quest for riches darkens the sense of right and wrong.

Antiphanes

Making a thousand decisions, even the wise will make a mistake.

Chinese proverb

For greed, all nature is too little.

Seneca

Adversity introduces a man to himself.

Unknown

If thou thinkest twice before thou speakest once, thou wilt speak twice the better for it.

William Penn

A bad workman blames his tools.

Chinese proverb

A good guitarist will play even if he has only one string.

South American proverb

One of the basic causes for all the trouble in the world today is that people talk too much and think too little. They act impulsively without thinking. I always try to think before I talk.

Margaret Chase Smith

He who asks a question may be a fool for five minutes; he who asks no questions stays a fool forever.

Chinese proverb

Anger and Bitterness

Never befriend the oppressed unless you are prepared to take on the oppressor.

Ogden Nash

All happy people are grateful. Ungrateful people cannot be happy. We tend to think that being unhappy leads people to complain, but it's truer to say that complaining leads to people becoming unhappy.

Dennis Prager

Anger makes dull men witty, but it keeps them poor.

Francis Bacon

Since the things we do determine the
character of life, no blessed person can
become unhappy, for he will never do those
things which are hateful and petty.

Aristotle

Resentment is like taking poison and waiting
for the other person to die.

Malachy McCourt

Keep away from people who try to belittle
your ambitions. Small people always do that,
but the really great make you feel that you,
too, can become great.

Mark Twain (Samuel Clemens)

Those who are free of resentful thoughts
surely find peace.

Buddha (Siddhartha Gautama)

Be patient and calm for no one can catch fish
in anger.

Herbert Hoover

Any man will usually get from other men just what he is expecting of them. If he is looking for friendship he will likely receive it. If his attitude is that of indifference, it will beget indifference. And if a man is looking for a fight, he will in all likelihood be accommodated in that.

John Richelsen

Friends may come and go, but enemies accumulate.

Thomas Hudson Jones

Anger is never without a reason, but seldom a good one.

Benjamin Franklin

The jealous are troublesome to others, but torment to themselves.

William Penn

He who angers you conquers you.

Elizabeth Kenny

I shall allow no man to belittle my soul by making me hate him.

Booker T. Washington

Instead of comparing our lot with that of those who are more fortunate than we are, we should compare it with the lot of the great majority of our fellow men. It then appears that we are among the privileged.

Helen Keller

Anger and intolerance are the enemies of correct understanding.

Mahatma Gandhi

Anger is a wind which blows out the lamp of the mind.

Robert Green Ingersoll

Never do anything when you are in a temper, for you will do everything wrong.

Baltasar Gracian

Bitterness is like cancer. It eats upon the host.
But anger is like fire. It burns it all clean.

Maya Angelou

Holding on to anger is like grasping a hot coal
with the intent of throwing it at someone else;
you are the one who gets burned.

Buddha

Anger is an acid that can do more harm to the
vessel in which it is stored than to anything on
which it is poured.

Mark Twain (Samuel Clemens)

A Call to Action

Actions lie louder than words.

Carolyn Wells

Deliberation is the function of the many;
action is the function of one.

Charles de Gaulle

The superior man is modest in his speech, but
exceeds in his actions.

Confucius

The superior man acts before he speaks, and
afterwards speaks according to his action.

Confucius

I have long since come to believe that people never mean half of what they say, and that it is best to disregard their talk and judge only their actions.

Dorothy Day

Happiness lies not in the mere possession of money. It lies in the joy of achievement, in the thrill of creative effort.

Franklin Delano Roosevelt

When it is obvious that the goals cannot be reached, don't adjust the goals, adjust the action steps.

Confucius

I have always thought the actions of men the best interpreters of their thoughts.

John Locke

I was seldom able to see an opportunity until it had ceased to be one.

Mark Twain (Samuel Clemens)

Don't be too timid and squeamish about your actions. All life is an experiment. The more experiments you make the better.

Ralph Waldo Emerson

Nothing will ever be attempted if all possible objections must be first overcome.

Samuel Johnson

Never confuse motion with action.

Benjamin Franklin

A real decision is measured by the fact that you've taken a new action. If there's no action, you haven't truly decided.

Tony Robbins

High achievers spot rich opportunities swiftly, make big decisions quickly and move into action immediately. Follow these principles and you can make your dreams come true.

Robert H. Schuller

Thought and theory must precede all salutary action; yet action is nobler in itself than either thought or theory.

Virginia Woolf

Words without actions are the assassins of idealism.

Herbert Hoover

Doubt, of whatever kind, can be ended by action alone.

Thomas Carlyle

Talk that does not end in any kind of action is better suppressed altogether.

Thomas Carlyle

He is the best man who, when making his plans, fears and reflects on everything that can happen to him, but in the moment of action is bold.

Herodotus

Be wary of the man who urges an action in
which he himself incurs no risk.

Seneca

Action is the foundational key to all success.

Pablo Picasso

Desire

The wise man will love; all others will desire.

Afranius

I count him braver who overcomes his desires than him who overcomes his enemies.

Aristotle

Let your desires be ruled by reason.

Cicero

Man is the only animal whose desires increase as they are fed; the only animal that is never satisfied.

Henry George

Manifest plainness,
Embrace simplicity,
Reduce selfishness,
Have few desires.

Lao-Tzu

There is no calamity greater than lavish
desires.
There is no greater guilt than discontentment.
And there is no greater disaster than greed.

Lao-Tzu

It is the nature of desire not to be satisfied,
and most men live only for the gratification of
it.

Aristotle

How helpless we are, like netted birds, when
we are caught by desire!

Belva Plain

He who desires is always poor.

Claudianus

A man who views the world the same at fifty as he did at twenty has wasted thirty years of his life.

Muhammad Ali

Don't ask yourself what the world needs; ask yourself what makes you come alive. And then go and do that. Because what the world needs is people who have come alive.

Howard Thurman

You can have anything you want if you want it desperately enough. You must want it with an exuberance that erupts through the skin and joins the energy that created the world.

Sheila Graham

The will to win, the desire to succeed, the urge to reach your full potential... these are the keys that will unlock the door to personal excellence.

Confucius

In order to succeed, your desire for success should be greater than your fear of failure.

Bill Cosby

Doing what is inside you: Confidence

The man who has confidence in himself gains
the confidence of others.

Hasidic Saying

I am not a has-been. I am a will be.

Lauren Bacall

Put your future in good hands - your own.

Unknown

It's lack of faith that makes people afraid of
meeting challenges, and I believed in myself.

Muhammad Ali

Believe in yourself! Have faith in your abilities! Without a humble but reasonable confidence in your own powers you cannot be successful or happy

Norman Vincent Peale

It's the repetition of affirmations that leads to belief. And once that belief becomes a deep conviction, things begin to happen.

Muhammad Ali

If I have lost confidence in myself, I have the universe against me.

Ralph Waldo Emerson

Self-confidence is the first requisite to great undertakings.

Samuel Johnson

My intent is simply to know my material so well that I'm very comfortable with it. Confidence, not perfection, is the goal.

Scott Berkun

Getting ahead in a difficult profession requires avid faith in yourself. That is why some people with mediocre talent, but with great inner drive, go much further than people with vastly superior talent.

Sophia Loren

Whatever you are by nature, keep to it; never desert your line of talent. Be what nature intended you for and you will succeed.

Sydney Smith

You can't connect the dots looking forward you can only connect them looking backwards. So you have to trust that the dots will somehow connect in your future. You have to trust in something: your gut, destiny, life, karma, whatever. Because believing that the dots will connect down the road will give you the confidence to follow your heart, even when it leads you off the well worn path.

Steve Jobs

If you have a talent, use it in every which way possible. Don't hoard it. Don't dole it out like a miser. Spend it lavishly like a millionaire intent on going broke.

Brendan Francis

Use what talents you possess: the woods would be very silent if no birds sang there except those that sang best.

Henry Van Dyke

We are always more anxious to be distinguished for a talent which we do not possess, than to be praised for the fifteen which we do possess.

Mark Twain (Samuel Clemens)

Education is the ability to listen to almost anything without losing your temper or your self-confidence.

Robert Frost

Nobody can make you feel inferior without your consent.

Eleanor Roosevelt

It's not who you are that holds you back, it's who you think you're not.

Unknown

If you hear a voice within you say "you cannot paint," then by all means paint, and that voice will be silenced.

Vincent Van Gogh

Confidence comes not from always being right but from not fearing to be wrong.

Peter T. Mcintyre

Confidence is preparation. Everything else is beyond your control.

Richard Kline

All you need in this life is ignorance and confidence; then success is sure.

Mark Twain (Samuel Clemens)

They are the weakest, however strong, who have no faith in themselves or their own powers.

Christian Bovee

Thousands of geniuses live and die undiscovered - either by themselves or by others.

Mark Twain (Samuel Clemens)

A great deal of talent is lost to the world for want of a little courage. Every day sends to their graves obscure men whose timidity prevented them from making a first effort.

Sydney Smith

The man who acquires the ability to take full possession of his own mind may take possession of anything else to which he is justly entitled.

Andrew Carnegie

You have brains in your head.

You have feet in your shoes.

You can steer yourself in any direction you choose.

You're on your own.

And you know what you know.

You are the guy who'll decide where to go.

Dr. Seuss

Without a humble but reasonable confidence in your own powers you cannot be successful or happy.

Norman Vincent Peale

If you really put a small value upon yourself, rest assured that the world will not raise your price.

Unknown

When there is no enemy within, the enemies outside cannot hurt you.

African Proverb

Persistence and Perseverance

Energy and persistence conquer all things.
Benjamin Franklin

Nothing in the world can take the place of
Persistence. Talent will not; nothing is more
common than unsuccessful men with talent.
Genius will not; unrewarded genius is almost a
proverb. Education will not; the world is full of
educated derelicts. Persistence and
determination alone are omnipotent. The
slogan 'Press On' has solved and always will
solve the problems of the human race.
Calvin Coolidge

You must keep sending work out; you must never let a manuscript do nothing but eat its head off in a drawer. You send that work out again and again, while you're working on another one. If you have talent, you will receive some measure of success - but only if you persist.

Isaac Asimov

That which we persist in doing becomes easier, not that the task itself has become easier, but that our ability to perform it has improved.

Ralph Waldo Emerson

Perseverance is not a long race; it is many short races one after the other.

Walter Elliot

Never let your head hang down. Never give up or sit down and grieve. Find another way.

Satchel Paige

I hated every minute of training, but I said, "Don't quit. Suffer now and live the rest of your life as a champion."

Muhammad Ali

Most of the important things in the world have been accomplished by people who have kept on trying when there seemed to be no hope at all.

Dale Carnegie

Stubbornly persist, and you will find that the limits of your stubbornness go well beyond the stubbornness of your limits.

Robert Brault

Most people never run far enough on their first wind to find out they've got a second.

William James

With ordinary talent and extraordinary perseverance, all things are attainable.

Thomas Foxwell Buxton

All of us have bad luck and good luck. The man who persists through the bad luck - who keeps right on going - is the man who is there when the good luck comes - and is ready to receive it.

Robert Collier

Remember that the man at the top of a mountain didn't just fall there.

Unknown

I am not discouraged because every wrong attempt discarded is a step forward.

Thomas Edison

You just can't beat the person who won't give up.

Babe Ruth

When you feel like giving up, remember why you held on for so long in the first place.

Anonymous

If we had no winter, the spring would not be so pleasant; if we did not sometimes taste of adversity, prosperity would not be so welcome.

Anne Bradstreet

Don't give up. There are too many nay-sayers out there who will try to discourage you. Don't listen to them. The only one who can make you give up is yourself.

Sidney Sheldon

Winners never quit, and quitters never win.

Vince Lombardi

People are always blaming circumstances for what they are. I don't believe in circumstances. The people who get ahead in this world are the people who get up and look for the circumstances they want, and if they can't find them, make them.

George Bernard Shaw

Trying and Succeeding

Formulate and stamp indelibly on your mind a mental picture of yourself as succeeding. Hold this picture tenaciously. Never permit it to fade. Your mind will seek to develop the picture...Do not build up obstacles in your imagination.

Norman Vincent Peale

I don't know the key to success, but the key to failure is trying to please everybody.

Bill Cosby

The person who makes a success of living is
the one who see his goal steadily and aims for
it unswervingly. That is dedication.

Cecil B. DeMille

Try not to be a man of success but rather to be
a man of value.

Albert Einstein

A great secret of success is to go through life
as a man who never gets used up.

Albert Schweitzer

Real success is finding your lifework in the
work that you love.

David McCullough

Success in business requires training and
discipline and hard work. But if you're not
frightened by these things, the opportunities
are just as great today as they ever were.

David Rockefeller

To follow, without halt, one aim: There's the
secret of success.

Anna Pavlova

Men are born to succeed, not fail.

Henry David Thoreau

I can't give you a sure-fire formula for success,
but I can give you a formula for failure: try to
please everybody all the time.

Herbert Bayard Swope

Success is walking from failure to failure with
no loss of enthusiasm

Sir Winston Churchill

Aim for success, not perfection. Never give up
your right to be wrong, because then you will
lose the ability to learn new things and move
forward with your life.

Dr. David M. Burns

It's not what happens to you that determines how far you will go in life; it is how you handle what happens to you.

Zig Ziglar

It is during our failures that we discover our true desire for success.

Kevin Ngo

The chief cause of failure and unhappiness is trading what we want most for what we want at the moment.

Unknown

It doesn't matter who you are, where you come from. The ability to triumph begins with you, always.

Oprah Winfrey

Things work out best for those who make the best of how things work out.

John Wooden

Some people dream of great accomplishments, while others stay awake and do them.

Anonymous

Let no feeling of discouragement prey upon you, and in the end you are sure to succeed.

Abraham Lincoln

Unless you try to do something beyond what you have already mastered, you will never grow.

Ronald E. Osborn

You may be disappointed if you fail, but you are doomed if you don't try.

Beverly Sills

None of the secrets of success will work unless you do.

Unknown

Nurture your thoughts

Nurture your mind with great thoughts; to believe in the heroic makes heroes.

Benjamin Disraeli

You are today where your thoughts have brought you; you will be tomorrow where your thoughts take you.

James Lane Allen

Our life is what our thoughts make it.

Marcus Aurelius

They are never alone that are accompanied with noble thoughts.

Sir Philip Sidney

Thoughts give birth to a creative force that is neither elemental nor sidereal. Thoughts create a new heaven, a new firmament, a new source of energy, from which new arts flow. When a man undertakes to create something, he establishes a new heaven, as it were and from it the work that he desires to create flows into him. For such is the immensity of man that he is greater than heaven and earth.

Philipus Aureolus Paracelsus

When I am attacked by gloomy thoughts, nothing helps me so much as running to my books. They quickly absorb me and banish the clouds from my mind.

Michel de Montaigne

The happiness of your life depends upon the quality of your thoughts, therefore guard accordingly; and take care that you entertain no notions unsuitable to virtue, and reasonable nature.

Marcus Aurelius Antoninus

Remember, happiness doesn't depend upon who you are or what you have; it depends solely upon what you think.

Dale Carnegie

The person who sends out positive thoughts activates the world around him positively and draws back to himself positive results.

Norman Vincent Peale

Watch your thoughts, they become words.
Watch your words, they become actions.
Watch your actions, they become habits.
Watch your habits, they become your character.
Watch your character, it becomes your destiny.

Unknown

A thought which, quartered, hath but one part wisdom and ever three parts coward.

William Shakespeare

If you fix in your mind the idea that your earning ability is limited, then indeed it is. You will never earn more than that self-set limit. The subconscious will create and maintain the limits you set.

Thomas D. Willhite

Your definite main goal is a set of thoughts···thoughts you control. Desire is an emotion which you create and control. Enthusiasm is a state of mind also subject to your control. Desire plus enthusiasm is the pulsating force to create things from thought.

Thomas D. Willhite

It's not what you look at that matters, it's what you see.

Henry David Thoreau

Only he is free who cultivates his own thoughts, and strives without fear to do justice to them.

Berthold Auerbach

Thoughts lead on to purposes; purposes go forth in action; actions form habits; habits decide character; and character fixes our destiny.

Unknown

In every work of genius we recognize our own rejected thoughts; they come back to us with a certain alienated majesty.

Ralph Waldo Emerson

Work

When you're doing the work you're meant to do, it feels right and every day is a bonus, regardless of what you're getting paid.

Oprah Winfrey

Never continue in a job you don't enjoy. If you're happy in what you're doing, you'll like yourself, you'll have inner peace. And if you have that, along with physical health, you will have had more success than you could possibly have imagined.

Johnny Carson

You've got to find what you love and that is as true for work as it is for lovers. Your work is going to fill a large part of your life and the only way to be truly satisfied is to do what you believe is great work. And the only way to do great work is to love what you do. If you haven't found it yet, keep looking and don't settle. As with all matters of the heart, you'll know when you've found it.

Steve Jobs

I'm a great believer in luck, and I find the harder I work the more I have of it.

Thomas Jefferson

When your work speaks for itself, don't interrupt.

Henry J. Kaiser

Derive happiness in oneself from a good day's work, from illuminating the fog that surrounds us.

Henri Matisse

You don't become great by trying to be great. You become great by wanting to do something, and then doing it so hard that you become great in the process.

Randall Munroe

Pleasure in the job puts perfection in the work.

Aristotle

You do your best work if you do a job that makes you happy.

Bob Ross

People forget how fast you did a job - but they remember how well you did it.

Howard Newton

Live neither in the past nor in the future, but let each day's work absorb your entire energies, and satisfy your widest ambition.

Sir William Osler

Real success is finding your lifework in the work that you love.

David McCullough

Folks who never do more than they're paid for, never get paid for any more than they do.

Elbert Hubbard

A professional is one who does his best work when he feels the least like working.

Frank Lloyd Wright

gDo not hire a man who does your work for money, but him who does it for love of it.

Henry David Thoreau

People who work sitting down get paid more than people who work standing up.

Ogden Nash

When you choose the paradigm of service, it turns everything you do from a job into a gift.

Oprah Winfrey

The more I want to get something done, the less I call it work.

Richard Bach

I long to accomplish a great and noble task, but it is my chief duty to accomplish humble tasks as though they were great and noble. The world is moved along, not only by the mighty shoves of its heroes, but also by the aggregate of the tiny pushes of each honest worker.

Helen Keller

It's not the hours you put in your work that counts, it's the work you put in the hours.

Sam Ewing

Work saves us from three great evils: boredom, vice and need.

Voltaire

The secret of greatness is simple: do better work than any other man in your field - and keep on doing it.

Wilfred A. Peterson

Far and away the best prize that life offers is the chance to work hard at work worth doing.

Theodore Roosevelt

Whenever it is in any way possible, every boy and girl should choose as his life work some occupation which he should like to do anyhow, even if he did not need the money.

William Lyon Phelps

Unless you are willing to drench yourself in your work beyond the capacity of the average man, you are just not cut out for positions at the top.

J.C. Penny

A leader is one who sees more than others see,
who sees farther than others see, and who
sees before others see.

Leroy Eims

Whoever does not love his work cannot hope
that it will please others.

Unknown

Be Inspired and Motivated

If you want to succeed in the world must make your own opportunities as you go on. The man who waits for some seventh wave to toss him on dry land will find that the seventh wave is a long time a coming. You can commit no greater folly than to sit by the roadside until someone comes along and invites you to ride with him to wealth or influence.

John B. Gough

Knowing is not enough; we must apply.
Willing is not enough; we must do.

Johann Wolfgang von Goethe

A creative man is motivated by the desire to achieve, not by the desire to beat others.

Ayn Rand

The man who has no imagination has no wings.

Muhammad Ali

Believe in yourself! Have faith in your abilities! Without a humble but reasonable confidence in your own powers you cannot be successful or happy.

Norman Vincent Peale

You can't build a reputation on what you are going to do.

Henry Ford

If you can dream it, you can do it.

Walt Disney

You are never too old to set another goal or to dream a new dream.

C. S. Lewis

He who is not courageous enough to take risks will accomplish nothing in life.

Muhammad Ali

Setting goals is the first step in turning the invisible into the visible.

Tony Robbins

The key is to keep company only with people who uplift you, whose presence calls forth your best.

Epictetus

If you want to conquer fear, don't sit home and think about it. Go out and get busy.

Dale Carnegie

The will to win, the desire to succeed, the urge to reach your full potential... these are the keys that will unlock the door to personal excellence.

Confucius

If you don't design your own life plan, chances are you'll fall into someone else's plan. And guess what they have planned for you? Not much.

Jim Rohn

If you want to succeed you should strike out on new paths, rather than travel the worn paths of accepted success.

John D. Rockefeller

Learn from the past, set vivid, detailed goals for the future, and live in the only moment of time over which you have any control: now.

Denis Waitley

If they can make penicillin out of moldy bread, they can sure make something out of you.

Muhammad Ali

Know or listen to those who know.

Baltasar Gracian

No matter how many goals you have achieved,
you must set your sights on a higher one.

Jessica Savitch

One way to keep momentum going is to have
constantly greater goals.

Michael Korda

People often say that motivation doesn't last.
Well, neither does bathing – that's why we
recommend it daily.

Zig Ziglar

Great Minds: Socrates

The only true wisdom is in knowing you know nothing.

Be kind, for everyone you meet is fighting a hard battle.

The unexamined life is not worth living.

Wonder is the beginning of wisdom.

I cannot teach anybody anything. I can only make them think

To find yourself, think for yourself.

Be slow to fall into friendship, but when you are in, continue firm and constant.

By all means marry; if you get a good wife, you'll become happy; if you get a bad one, you'll become a philosopher.

The only good is knowledge and the only evil is ignorance.

Esteemed friend, citizen of Athens, the greatest city in the world, so outstanding in both intelligence and power, aren't you ashamed to care so much to make all the money you can, and to advance your reputation and prestige--while for truth and wisdom and the improvement of your soul you have no care or worry?

If you don't get what you want, you suffer; if you get what you don't want, you suffer; even when you get exactly what you want, you still suffer because you can't hold on to it forever. Your mind is your predicament. It wants to be free of change. Free of pain, free of the obligations of life and death. But change is law and no amount of pretending will alter that reality.

Education is the kindling of a flame, not the filling of a vessel.

Our youth now love luxury. They have bad manners, contempt for authority; they show disrespect for their elders and love chatter in place of exercise; they no longer rise when elders enter the room; they contradict their parents, chatter before company; gobble up their food and tyrannize their teachers.

I am not an Athenian nor a Greek, but a citizen of the world.

Prefer knowledge to wealth, for the one is transitory, the other perpetual

Let him who would move the world first move himself.

When the debate is lost, slander becomes the tool of the loser.

Thou shouldst eat to live; not live to eat.

The secret of happiness, you see, is not found in seeking more, but in developing the capacity to enjoy less.

Envy is the ulcer of the soul.

Employ your time in improving yourself by other men's writings so that you shall come easily by what others have labored hard for.

Sometimes you put walls up not to keep people out, but to see who cares enough to break them down.

Beware of the barrenness of a busy life.

Be of good cheer about death, and know this of a truth, that no evil can happen to a good man, either in life or after death.

The secret of change is to focus all of your energy, not on fighting the old, but on building the new.

The really important thing is not to live, but to live well. And to live well meant, along with more enjoyable things in life, to live according to your principles.

Strong minds discuss ideas, average minds discuss events, weak minds discuss people.

True wisdom comes to each of us when we realize how little we understand about life, ourselves, and the world around us.

Great Minds: Plato

Every heart sings a song, incomplete, until another heart whispers back. Those who wish to sing always find a song. At the touch of a lover, everyone becomes a poet.

There is truth in wine and children

The price good men pay for indifference to public affairs is to be ruled by evil men.

Love is a serious mental disease.

There are three classes of men; lovers of wisdom, lovers of honor, and lovers of gain.

I'm trying to think, don't confuse me with facts.

Education is teaching our children to desire the right things.

Good actions give strength to ourselves and inspire good actions in others.

Death is not the worst that can happen to men.

Character is simply habit long continued.

Necessity is the mother of invention.

Love is the pursuit of the whole.

Music gives a soul to the universe, wings to the mind, flight to the imagination and life to everything.

Wise men speak because they have something to say; fools because they have to say something.

Only the dead have seen the end of war.

Do not train a child to learn by force or harshness; but direct them to it by what amuses their minds, so that you may be better able to discover with accuracy the peculiar bent of the genius of each.

You can discover more about a person in an hour of play than in a year of conversation.

Great Minds: Aristotle

Knowing yourself is the beginning of all
wisdom.

What is a friend? A single soul dwelling in two
bodies.

A friend to all is a friend to none.

Those who educate children well are more to
be honored than they who produce them; for

these only gave them life, those the art of living well.

Patience is bitter, but its fruit is sweet.

It is the mark of an educated mind to be able to entertain a thought without accepting it.

We are what we repeatedly do. Excellence, then, is not an act, but a habit.

Happiness depends upon ourselves.

Educating the mind without educating the heart is no education at all.

To avoid criticism say nothing, do nothing, be nothing.

Wishing to be friends is quick work, but friendship is a slow ripening fruit.

Happiness is the meaning and the purpose of life, the whole aim and end of human existence.

To perceive is to suffer.

Anybody can become angry — that is easy, but to be angry with the right person and to the right degree and at the right time and for the right purpose, and in the right way — that is not within everybody's power and is not easy.

The educated differ from the uneducated as much as the living differ from the dead.

Excellence is never an accident. It is always the result of high intention, sincere effort, and intelligent execution; it represents the wise choice of many alternatives - choice, not chance, determines your destiny.

He who has overcome his fears will truly be
free.

Great Minds: Nietzsche

Man is the cruelest animal.

A good writer possesses not only his own spirit but also the spirit of his friends.

Without music, life would be a mistake.

That which does not kill us makes us stronger.

It is not a lack of love, but a lack of friendship that makes unhappy marriages.

I'm not upset that you lied to me, I'm upset that from now on I can't believe you.

It is hard enough to remember my opinions, without also remembering my reasons for them!

You have your way. I have my way. As for the right way, the correct way, and the only way, it does not exist.

The surest way to corrupt a youth is to instruct him to hold in higher esteem those who think alike than those who think differently.

What does your conscience say? — 'You should become the person you are'.

All I need is a sheet of paper and something to write with, and then I can turn the world upside down.

There is always some madness in love. But there is also always some reason in madness.

In heaven, all the interesting people are missing.

And those who were seen dancing were thought to be insane by those who could not hear the music.

Whoever fights monsters should see to it that in the process he does not become a monster. And if you gaze long enough into an abyss, the abyss will gaze back into you.

We should consider every day lost on which we have not danced at least once.

The individual has always had to struggle to keep from being overwhelmed by the tribe. If you try it, you will be lonely often, and sometimes frightened. But no price is too high to pay for the privilege of owning yourself.

Sometimes people don't want to hear the truth because they don't want their illusions destroyed.

The man of knowledge must be able not only to love his enemies but also to hate his friends.

I cannot believe in a God who wants to be praised all the time.

I would believe only in a God that knows how to dance.

The advantage of a bad memory is that one enjoys several times the same good things for the first time.

Faith: not wanting to know what the truth is.

What labels me, negates me.

He who would learn to fly one day must first learn to walk and run and climb and dance; one cannot fly into flying.

There are two different types of people in the world, those who want to know, and those who want to believe.

Perhaps I know best why it is man alone who laughs; he alone suffers so deeply that he had to invent laughter.

Great Minds: Gandhi

Be the change that you wish to see in the world.

Live as if you were to die tomorrow. Learn as if you were to live forever.

An eye for an eye will only make the whole world blind.

When I despair, I remember that all through history the way of truth and love have always won. There have been tyrants and murderers, and for a time, they can seem invincible, but in the end, they always fall. Think of it--always.

Where there is love there is life.

Freedom is not worth having if it does not include the freedom to make mistakes.

Nobody can hurt me without my permission.

A man is but the product of his thoughts. What he thinks, he becomes.

Great Minds: Cicero

Times are bad. Children no longer obey their parents, and everyone is writing a book.

Friendship improves happiness, and abates misery, by doubling our joys, and dividing our grief

A room without books is like a body without a soul.

If you have a garden and a library, you have everything you need.

To be ignorant of what occurred before you were born is to remain always a child. For what is the worth of human life, unless it is woven into the life of our ancestors by the records of history?

Six mistakes mankind keeps making century after century:
Believing that personal gain is made by crushing others
Worrying about things that cannot be changed or corrected
Insisting that a thing is impossible because we cannot accomplish it
Refusing to set aside trivial preferences
Neglecting development and refinement of the mind

Attempting to compel others to believe and
live as we do

To add a library to a house is to give that
house a soul.

Laws are silent in times of war.

If we are not ashamed to think it, we should
not be ashamed to say it.

The life given us, by nature is short; but the
memory of a well-spent life is eternal.

Great Minds: Einstein

Insanity is doing the same thing, over and over again, but expecting different results.

Two things are infinite: the universe and human stupidity; and I'm not sure about the universe.

There are only two ways to live your life. One is as though nothing is a miracle. The other is as though everything is a miracle.

I am enough of an artist to draw freely upon my imagination. Imagination is more important than knowledge. Knowledge is limited. Imagination encircles the world.

If you can't explain it to a six year old, you don't understand it yourself.

If you want your children to be intelligent, read them fairy tales. If you want them to be more intelligent, read them more fairy tales.

If a cluttered desk is a sign of a cluttered mind, of what, then, is an empty desk a sign?

The difference between genius and stupidity is; genius has its limits.

Anyone who has never made a mistake has never tried anything new.

Life is like riding a bicycle. To keep your balance, you must keep moving.

I speak to everyone in the same way, whether he is the garbage man or the president of the university.

A clever person solves a problem. A wise person avoids it.

Everybody is a genius. But if you judge a fish by its ability to climb a tree, it will live its whole life believing that it is stupid.

Education is what remains after one has forgotten what one has learned in school.

Try not to become a man of success. Rather become a man of value.

The best way to cheer yourself is to cheer somebody else up.

What is right is not always popular and what
is popular is not always right.

Great Minds: Camus

Don't walk behind me; I may not lead. Don't walk in front of me; I may not follow. Just walk beside me and be my friend.

You will never be happy if you continue to search for what happiness consists of. You will never live if you are looking for the meaning of life.

Live to the point of tears.

Blessed are the hearts that can bend; they shall never be broken.

There are causes worth dying for, but none worth killing for.

The only way to deal with an unfree world is to become so absolutely free that your very existence is an act of rebellion.

To be happy, we must not be too concerned with others.

The purpose of a writer is to keep civilization from destroying itself.

Always go too far, because that's where you'll find the truth

I would rather live my life as if there is a God and die to find out there isn't, than live my life as if there isn't and die to find out there is.

Freedom is nothing but a chance to be better.

Always there comes an hour when one is weary of one's work and devotion to duty, and all one craves for is a loved face, the warmth and wonder of a loving heart.

Great Minds: Confucius

If you make a mistake and do not correct it,
this is called a mistake.

Before you embark on a journey of revenge,
dig two graves.

It is not the failure of others to appreciate
your abilities that should trouble you, but
rather your failure to appreciate theirs.

He who knows all the answers has not been
asked all the questions.

Our greatest glory is not in never falling, but in rising every time we fall.

To be wronged is nothing, unless you continue to remember it.

Life is really simple, but we insist on making it complicated.

Wherever you go, go with all your heart.

It does not matter how slowly you go as long as you do not stop.

The man who moves a mountain begins by carrying away small stones.

What the superior man seeks is in himself; what the small man seeks is in others.

Only the wisest and stupidest of men never change.

What to do next

Carry this book with you, or have it nearby. Turn to the appropriate chapter when you need help deciding what to do, need a little motivation, or need help deciding which is the right path to take.

Set goals for yourself. Make them specific achievable goals with realistic dates. Setting goals that are too far outside of your reach will only frustrate you and cause you to give up. To achieve a major goal, set little goals that you can achieve in a reasonable timeframe.

If you set goals without a specific date, you will never reach those goals, or reach them much later than if you had set an achievable target date. Setting dates helps you stay focused and helps you attain those goals.

Use the blank pages to write down your goals, and the spaces between the quotes to jot down any thoughts the quotes inspire. This will help to remind you of what is important to you whenever you refer to the book.